Smithsonian

DIGGING FOR BRACHIOSAURUS

BY THOMAS R. HOLTZ JR., Ph.D.

A Discovery TIMELINE

CAPSTONE PRESS
a capstone imprint

Capstone Press
1710 Roe Crest Drive
North Mankato, Minnesota 56003
www.capstonepub.com

Our very special thanks to Mike Brett-Surman, PhD, Museum Specialist for Fossil Dinosaurs, Reptiles, Amphibians, and Fish at the National Museum of Natural History, Smithsonian Institution, for his curatorial review. Capstone would also like to thank Kealy Wilson, Product Development Manager, and the following at Smithsonian Enterprises: Ellen Nanney, Licensing Manager; Brigid Ferraro, Vice President, Education and Consumer Products; Carol LeBlanc, Senior Vice President, Education and Consumer Products.

Library of Congress Cataloging-in-Publication Data
Holtz, Thomas R., 1965– author.
Digging for Brachiosaurus: a discovery timeline/by Thomas R. Holtz, Jr.
pages cm. —(Smithsonian. Dinosaur discovery timelines)
Summary: "Provides an annotated timeline of the discovery of Brachiosaurus, including details on the scientists, dig sites, fossils, and other findings that have shaped our knowledge of this dinosaur"—Provided by publisher.
Audience: Ages 8–12.
Audience: Grade 2–6.
Includes bibliographical references and index.
ISBN 978-1-4914-2123-9 (library binding) ISBN 978-1-4914-2364-6 (paperback)
1. Brachiosaurus—Juvenile literature. 2. Dinosaurs—Juvenile literature.
3. Paleontology—History—Juvenile literature. I. Title.
QE862.S3H6532 2015
567.913—dc23 2014024628

Editorial Credits
Kristen Mohn, editor; Lori Bye and Aruna Rangarajan, designers; Wanda Winch and Kelly Garvin, media researchers; Kathy McColley, production specialist

Photo Credits
Alamy: Stocktrek Images/Nobumichi Tanura, 17 (right); AP Images: Museo Paletontologico Egidio Feruglio, 24 (r); Ben and Jessie Stallings, 15; Corbis: Bettmann, 20, Louie Psihoyos, 13 (left), 17 (l), 23 (l); Courtesy of Dr. Daniela Schwarz-Wings, 26 (r); Garden Park Paleontology Society, Canon City, CO, 12 (r); Getty Images: De Agostini/De Agostini Picture Library, 7, Field Museum Library, 9 (r); Jon Hughes, cover, 1, 21 (r), 25 (top), 29; Library of Congress: Prints and Photographs Division, 9 (l); Mathew Wedel, PhD, Western University of Health Sciences, 14 (bottom left); ©Museum für Naturkunde, Berlin,16 (r); National Park Service, Dinosaur National Monument, 19 (b) Newscom: EPA/Stephanie Pilick, 13 (r); Photo by Christophe Hendrickx, 18 (bottom); Photo by Heinrich Mallison, 26 (l); Royal Gorge Regional Museum & History Center, 12 (l); Science Source, 6, 10 (top right), Francois Gohier, 5, 14 (r), 21 (l), 22 (b), John Kaprielian, 24 (bl), Joyce Photographics, 10 (b) Julius T. Csotonyl, 25 (b), Laurie O'Keefe, 8 (bl), Warren Photographic/Kim Taylor, 11 (r); Shutterstock: Catmando, 27, backcover, Luis Molinero, textured beige design, Michael Rosskothen, 19 (tr), Paganin, 19 (tl), Robert Adrian Hillman, blue, smoky designs; Thomas Boylan, 11 (l); Wikimedia/ LadyofHats, 23 (r), John A. Ryder, 8 (br)

Printed in Canada.
092014 008478FRS15

Table of Contents

BRACHIOSAURUS

Dinosaurs are famous for being big. (Actually, some dinosaurs were very small, but the big ones are more famous!) For a long time, the biggest dinosaur we knew about was *Brachiosaurus*.

No humans lived at the same time as *Brachiosaurus*, so how do we know about this creature? We know about it because scientists have found and studied its fossils. Fossils are evidence of life from the geologic past, such as bones, teeth, footprints, and other remains that are preserved in rocks. Paleontologists—people who study fossils—use these remains to piece together the lives and habits of ancient creatures.

Usually, paleontologists don't start with a complete skeleton of a dinosaur. Instead, they study the animal rock by rock, bone by bone. And this is how we learned about *Brachiosaurus*.

In this book we journey through the discoveries that led to our understanding of *Brachiosaurus* and its relatives. First, we have to look at the discovery of long-necked dinosaurs in general. When these animals' bones were first found, no one knew what on Earth they were.

skull of *Camarasaurus*, a smaller relative of *Brachiosaurus*

Chipping Norton, Oxfordshire, United Kingdom: *Whale Lizards?*

1841
Paleontologist Sir Richard Owen names Kingdon's bones *Cetiosaurus* ("whale lizard"). He thinks they are from an extinct gigantic seagoing reptile. This is the first find of a *Brachiosaurus* relative, but it will take many more discoveries to figure that out.

1825
Fossil collector John Kingdon is prospecting for bones in quarries in the Chipping Norton region. He finds vertebrae (backbones) and leg bones. He thinks they might be from a whale or a giant crocodile.

Cetiosaurus

1842
Owen coins the word "dinosaur" to describe a group of large, extinct reptiles. He doesn't know that *Cetiosaurus* is actually one of the creatures he just named. He still thinks it is a sea animal, while his newly named dinosaurs were land animals.

1868–1870
Scientists find more specimens of *Cetiosaurus*. None of the skeletons are complete.

Garden Park Fossil Area, Colorado: *An American Giant*

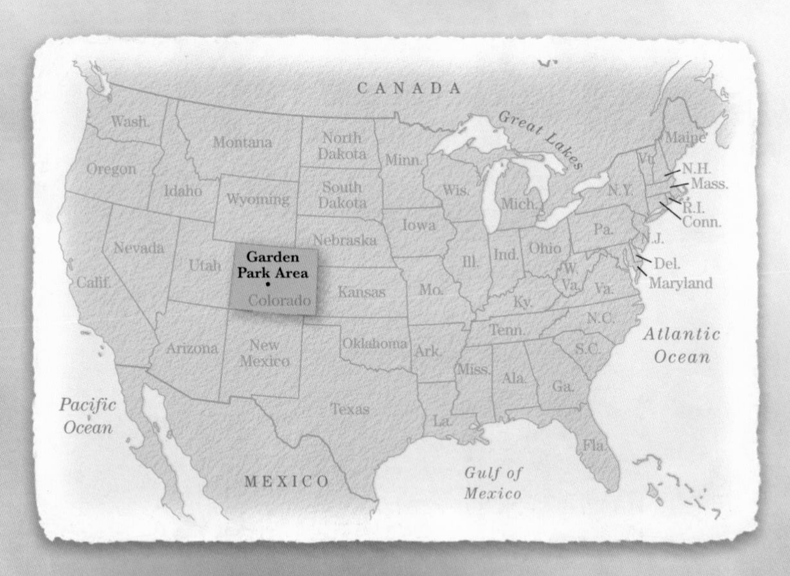

John Ryder's *Camarasaurus* drawing

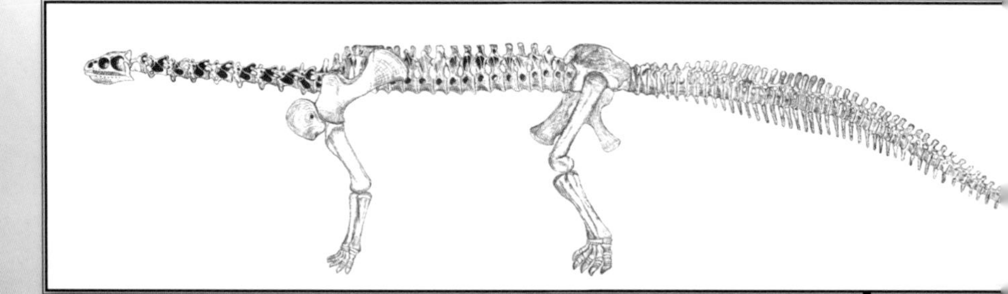

Spring 1877
Colorado schoolteacher Oramel W. Lucas finds scattered vertebrae. He and his family of pioneers dig them up. The bones have big, open spaces in them. He sends letters to Edward Drinker Cope and Othniel Charles Marsh, America's most famous paleontologists. Cope buys the bones from Lucas and names the creature *Camarasaurus* ("chambered lizard").

December 21, 1877
The first-ever drawing of a long-necked dinosaur skeleton—a *Camarasaurus*—is shown at a meeting of the American Philosophical Society. The drawing, created by illustrator John Ryder, is based on an incomplete skeleton, but it shows that *Camarasaurus* was bigger than any land animal living today.

Camarasaurus

1877
Cope's rival, Marsh, finds an incomplete skeleton. He names it *Morosaurus* ("stupid lizard"), because it had a very small brain for its body size. It turns out to be another species of *Camarasaurus*.

Charles W. Gilmore at work at the Smithsonian in 1938

1925
Smithsonian paleontologist Charles W. Gilmore finds the first complete *Camarasaurus* skeleton. It is a young dinosaur, not much bigger than a rhino.

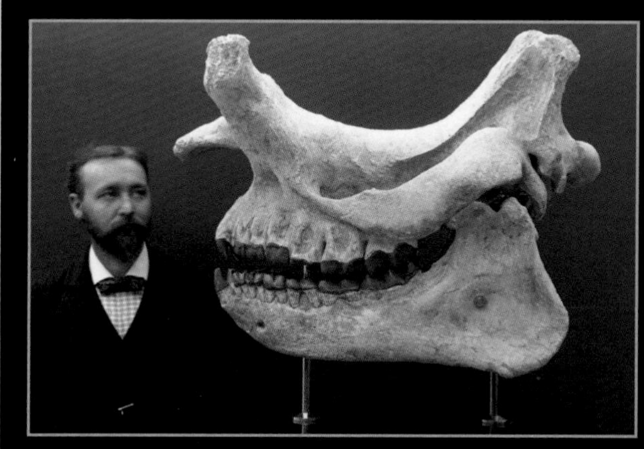

EXPERT: *Elmer Riggs*

Elmer Samuel Riggs (1869–1963) was the paleontologist who discovered and named *Brachiosaurus*. For most of his life he worked for the Field Museum of Natural History in Chicago. Although he is most famous for his work on *Brachiosaurus* and its relatives, Riggs mostly did research on fossil mammals.

When Riggs was a college student, his professors noticed that he was very good at finding fossils and planning digs in the field. The Field Museum hired him to lead fossil-hunting trips around the American West and South America.

Riggs was very interested in bringing paleontology and geology students out into the field. He taught them the skills they needed to discover and understand new fossils.

It is important for scientists to get their ideas out to people in the public. Riggs was famous for being a good speaker. Many schools and clubs invited him to speak about his discoveries. He kept on giving talks even after he retired.

Across the American West: *More Jurassic Giants*

Marsh's expedition team

Summer 1877

Near Jefferson County, Colorado, naturalist Arthur Lakes finds the nearly complete skeleton of a dinosaur that is larger than *Camarasaurus*. Marsh later names it *Apatosaurus* ("deceptive lizard") because scientists first thought it was going to be a different kind of reptile.

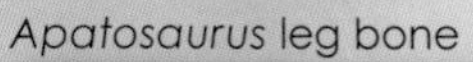

Apatosaurus leg bone

September 1877

Another partial skeleton of a big dinosaur is found at Cañon City, Colorado, by geologist Benjamin Mudge and paleontologist Samuel Williston, exploring for Marsh. It is longer and more slender than *Apatosaurus*. Because of the two-way split of the bones under the tail, Marsh later names it *Diplodocus* ("double-beam").

Apatosaurus/Brontosaurus

1878

At Como Bluff, Wyoming, yet another giant specimen is found. Marsh names it *Brontosaurus* ("thunder lizard"). Over the next several decades, many more skeletons of giant dinosaurs are found in Jurassic rocks of Colorado, Wyoming, Utah, and nearby states. Marsh names the entire group of giant, long-necked dinosaurs Sauropoda ("lizard feet").

1903

Paleontologist Elmer Riggs reexamines the bones of *Brontosaurus*. He shows that it is a type of *Apatosaurus* rather than its own type of dinosaur. Many other scientists disagree with Riggs. Until 1975 they continue using the name *Brontosaurus*.

Como Bluff, Wyoming

Garden Park Fossil Area, Colorado: *A Mystery Skull*

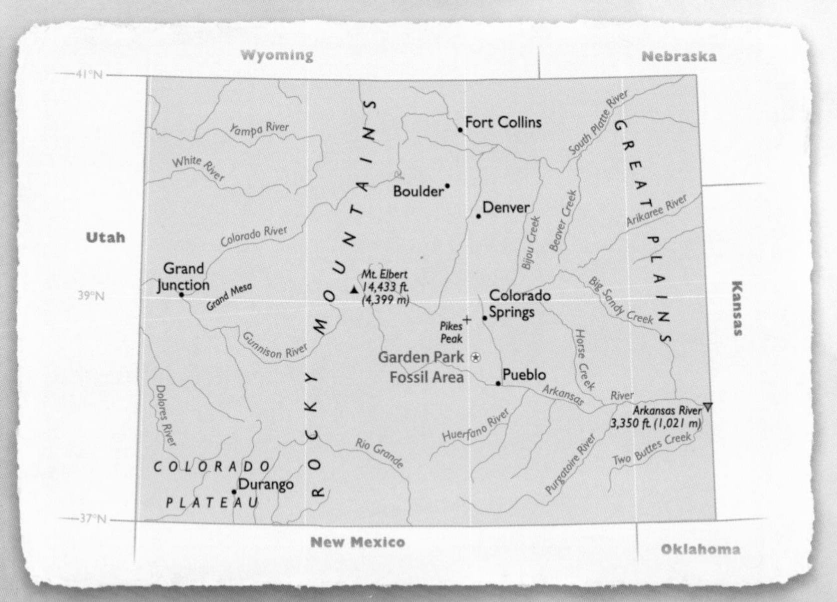

1883
Marshall P. Felch, collecting for Marsh, finds a partial skull of a sauropod. This creature is very big. Its skull is different from both *Camarasaurus*' short, blunt skull and *Diplodocus*' long, horselike skull.

Garden Park Fossil Area

Marshall P. Felch

1891
Marsh decides that since Felch's specimen is the biggest sauropod skull, and *Brontosaurus* is the biggest known sauropod, then Felch's find must be a *Brontosaurus*. From now until the 1970s, pictures and mounted skeletons of *Brontosaurus* follow Marsh's idea. But Felch's skull will remain unstudied all this time.

Jack McIntosh with an *Apatosaurus* skeleton

1998
Paleontologists Kenneth Carpenter and Virginia Tidwell finally describe Felch's skull in detail. Earlier they had put together a model of the skull, which is now on display at the Denver Museum of Nature and Science.

model of a *Brachiosaurus* skull

1975
Paleontologists Jack McIntosh and David Berman find the actual skull of *Apatosaurus* (*Brontosaurus*), which is much more like that of *Diplodocus*. McIntosh recognizes that the Felch skull is actually from *Brachiosaurus*. Thus, Felch's 1883 skull find is the first fossil of *Brachiosaurus* ever discovered!

Fruita, Colorado: *Elmer's Giant*

JULY 4, 1900
Field collector H. William Menke and his boss, Elmer Riggs, find bones from a truly giant sauropod near Fruita, Colorado.

Fruita, Colorado

1903
Riggs studies the bones from 1900. He finds that the dinosaur's front legs are longer than its hind legs. This is unusual in dinosaurs, and it is described as being built "uphill." Riggs names it *Brachiosaurus* ("arm lizard") in honor of its long "arms." This skeleton is incomplete, but the bones are bigger than those of the biggest *Apatosaurus* or *Diplodocus*. (At the time, these are the biggest known dinosaurs.) So *Brachiosaurus* takes over as the biggest dinosaur of all.

Brachiosaurus, built "uphill"

1994
Scientists make a plastic model skeleton by combining the bones of Riggs' specimen and those of an African brachiosaur. This is the first *Brachiosaurus* skeleton mounted in the United States.

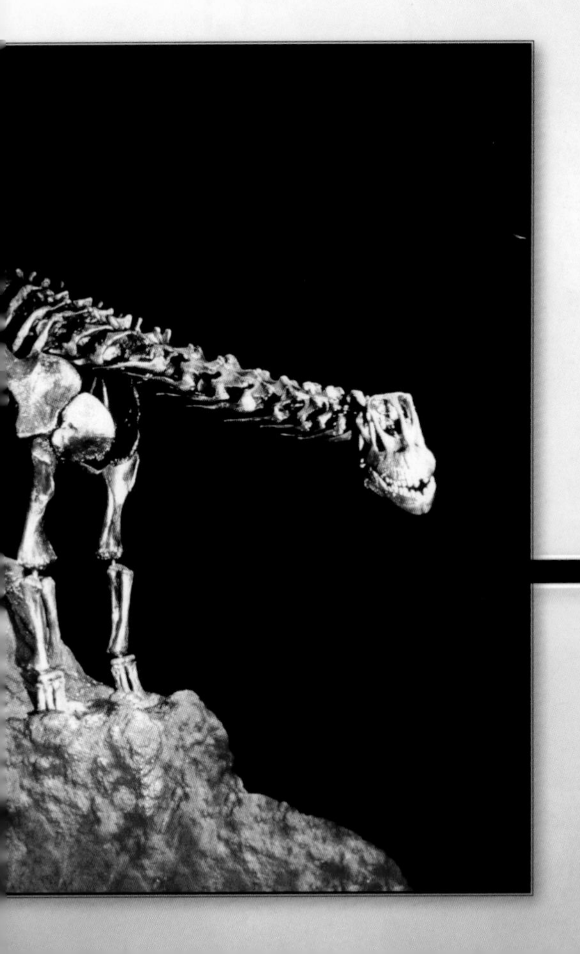

1999
The plastic *Brachiosaurus* skeleton is moved from the Field Museum of Natural History in Chicago to Chicago's O'Hare International Airport. It stands there today.

Tendaguru Hill, Tanzania: *An African Brachiosaur*

1909
The first specimens of a giant sauropod are found in what is now the country of Tanzania.

1914
Paleontologist Werner Janensch describes the skeletons from Africa as a new species of *Brachiosaurus*. Scientists confirm that the arms are much longer than the legs. The African fossils include the best brachiosaur skull ever found.

quarry at Tendaguru Hill

Giraffatitan

1937
A skeleton of the African *Brachiosaurus* is mounted in Berlin, Germany. For many decades, it is the largest and tallest dinosaur skeleton on display anywhere in the world.

1988
Paleontologist Gregory S. Paul compares the African *Brachiosaurus* species with the North American one. He claims that the African one is too different to be considered *Brachiosaurus*. He gives it a new name: *Giraffatitan* ("giant giraffe").

2009
Paleontologist Michael Taylor confirms that *Giraffatitan* and *Brachiosaurus* are different.

Around the World: *Brachiosaurus' Cousins*

1999
In Utah Tidwell and her team find a *Brachiosaurus*-like dinosaur from the Cretaceous Period. It is named *Cedarosaurus* after the Cedar Mountain Formation, the rock formation where the fossil was found.

1957
The Lourinhã specimen is described as a kind of *Brachiosaurus*.

1947
Remains of a giant Jurassic sauropod are discovered in Lourinhã, Portugal.

Lourinhã, Portugal

Europasaurus

2006

A "dwarf" brachiosaur is found in the Jurassic rocks of Germany. The adults were not much bigger than a modern horse. It is named *Europasaurus* ("Europe lizard"). It was small most likely because it lived on islands, where being a giant would lead to starvation.

2010

A nearly complete fossil brachiosaur skull is found in Cretaceous rocks of Utah. These rocks are younger than the rocks of *Cedarosaurus*. The new dinosaur is named *Abydosaurus*.

Abydosaurus skull

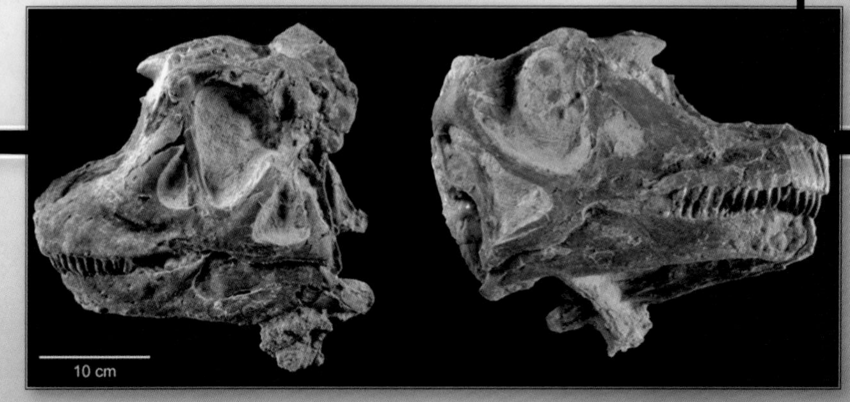

2003

The Lourinhã dinosaur gets its own name: *Lusotitan* ("Portuguese giant"). Like *Brachiosaurus* and *Giraffatitan*, *Lusotitan* has long, slender front legs.

Glen Rose, Texas: *Tracks of a Brachiosaur*

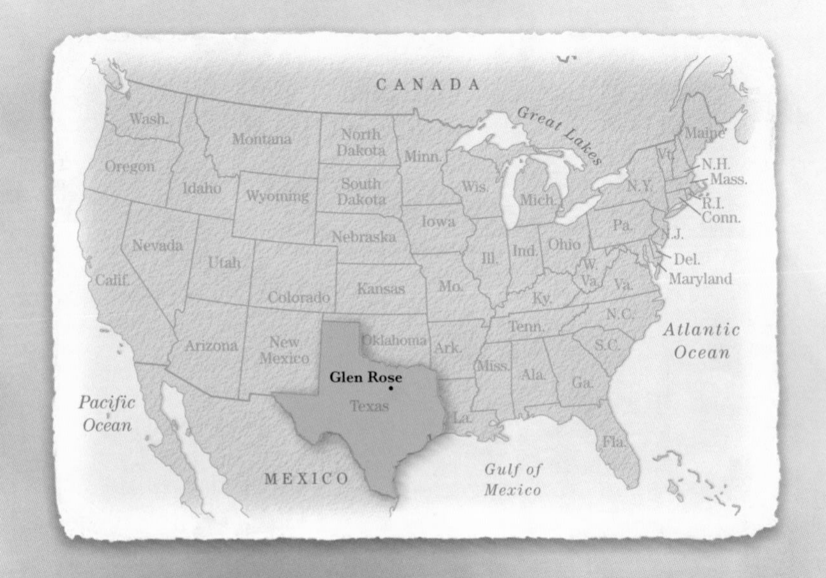

Roland T. Bird measuring a dinosaur footprint

1938
In Glen Rose, Texas, near the Paluxy River, Roland T. Bird discovers the first definite sauropod tracks ever found. Some of the tracks show that a big meat-eating dinosaur was chasing the sauropod!

1989
Paleontologist James Farlow studies the tracks, which he knows were made after *Brachiosaurus* became extinct. However, Farlow shows that the feet that made these tracks are more like those of *Brachiosaurus* than any other known dinosaur.

2000

Paleontologist Mathew Wedel and his team describe *Sauroposeidon* ("earthquake-god lizard"). This *Brachiosaurus*-like dinosaur is from the right age and region to have made the tracks Bird found. Almost all the evidence now suggests that the Paluxy tracks are from *Sauroposeidon*. *Sauroposeidon* turns out to be even bigger than *Brachiosaurus*.

Sauroposeidon

Paluxy tracks

2014

Farlow uses new 3-D computer and photography techniques to put together the whole *Sauroposeidon* trackway. Parts of it have been separated or lost over the years.

Dry Mesa Dinosaur Quarry, Colorado: *Dinosaur Jim's Giants*

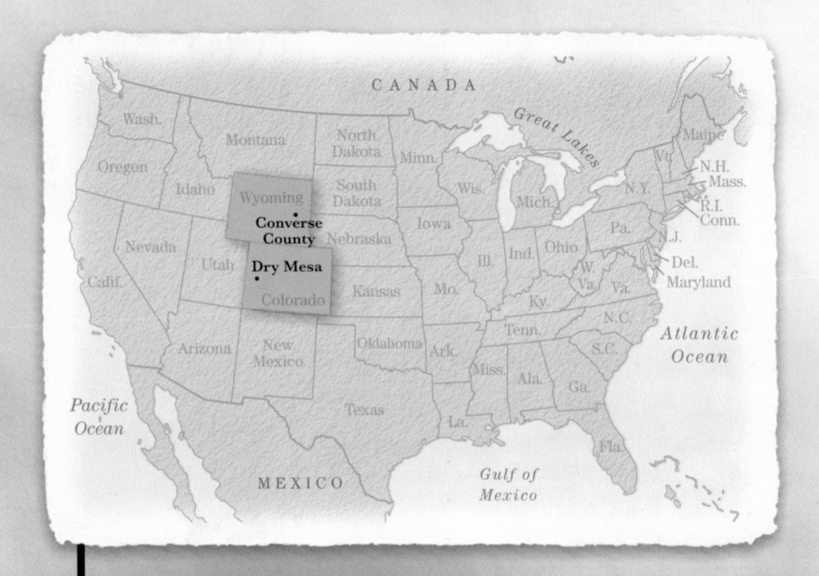

1971
Dinosaur hunters Daniel and Vivian Jones and paleontologist James "Dinosaur Jim" Jensen start to explore a new dinosaur quarry called Dry Mesa near Delta, Colorado.

1972
Jensen and the Joneses find the bones of giant sauropods. Some are from a giant *Diplodocus*-like dinosaur that they name *Supersaurus*. Other bones seem to be even bigger. These bones come from a *Brachiosaurus*-like dinosaur that they name *Ultrasaurus*.

paleontology student at Dry Mesa

James Jensen with a *Brachiosaurus* leg

1996

Paleontologist Brian Curtice shows that the *Brachiosaurus*-like bones actually come from a very big *Brachiosaurus*, so the name *Ultrasaurus* is no longer used.

2007

On the other hand, Dinosaur Jim's team was right about *Supersaurus*. The discovery of a new *Supersaurus* specimen in Converse County, Wyoming, confirms that it is a huge, *Diplodocus*-like dinosaur.

Supersaurus

North America and Argentina: *Bigger than Brachiosaurus*

1893
Paleontologist Richard Lydekker finds and names *Argyrosaurus* ("silver lizard") from Cretaceous rocks in Argentina. All he found was a front leg, but it shows that there were sauropods much bigger than *Apatosaurus*. Lydekker's discovery is ignored for several decades.

1987
A giant dinosaur leg bone is found in Cretaceous rocks of Argentina. It is so big that the discoverers think it is a tree trunk!

paleontologist Pablo Puerta

Alamosaurus

1922
Charles Gilmore names *Alamosaurus* ("lizard from the Ojo Alamo Formation"). This sauropod comes from the end of the Age of Dinosaurs in New Mexico. More fossils are found in Texas and Utah.

Argentinosaurus

2011
New fossils show that the original *Alamosaurus* specimens were young dinosaurs. A fully grown *Alamosaurus* was much bigger than *Brachiosaurus*.

1993
The dinosaur with the huge leg bone is named *Argentinosaurus* ("Argentina lizard"). It is one of the biggest dinosaurs ever found.

2001
Yet another giant sauropod from the Cretaceous Period of Argentina is named *Puertasaurus*, in honor of discoverer Pablo Puerta. Although *Brachiosaurus* was long famous as the largest dinosaur, it clearly was not.

2000
A truly gigantic dinosaur skeleton is found in Argentina. It takes many years to excavate. This creature is eventually named *Futalognkosaurus* ("big chief lizard") in 2007. This is the biggest dinosaur for which most of the skeleton (about 70 percent) has been discovered.

Futalognkosaurus

Shell, Wyoming: *A Baby Brachiosaurus!*

Daniela Schwarz-Wings at a cliff from the Cretaceous Period

2005
A small sauropod skeleton is found. One of the field workers names it Toni.

Toni on display at a museum in Switzerland

2007
Paleontologist Daniela Schwarz-Wings and her team describe Toni's skeleton. They think it is a baby *Diplodocus* or *Diplodocus* relative. The dinosaur was probably about 6 feet (less than 2 meters) long. Most of that length came from the tail and neck.

Brachiosaurus group

2012

A new study of Toni shows that it isn't a *Diplodocus* at all. It is a baby *Brachiosaurus*! Baby *Brachiosauruses* had long arms, but not as long compared to its legs as the adult arms. So, like many animals, *Brachiosaurus* changed shape as well as size as it grew older.

About *Brachiosaurus*

Length: 85 feet (26 m)

Height: 30 feet (9 m)

Weight: 32 tons (29 metric tons)

Age: 156 to 147 million years ago, in the later part of the Jurassic Period

Location: Western North America

Diet: Plants (especially trees). An adult *Brachiosaurus* had to eat hundreds of pounds of leaves and twigs every day. Being built uphill, with longer arms than legs, it could easily feed high in trees, without competing for plants with the lower-feeding *Diplodocus* and *Camarasaurus*.

Distinctive features: Front legs were longer than back legs. For this reason, it probably could not stand on its hind legs.

Enemies: An adult *Brachiosaurus* had few enemies, but as it was growing up it had to battle meat eaters, from the small *Ornitholestes* to giants like *Ceratosaurus*, *Allosaurus*, and *Torvosaurus*.

Relatives: Closely related to *Giraffatitan* of eastern Africa and *Lusotitan* of Portugal

Hearing: Based on the shape of its inner ear, *Brachiosaurus* heard sounds that were much lower than any human could hear.

Glossary

Brachiosaur—a member of the *Brachiosaurus* group

Cretaceous Period—the span of geologic time from 145 to 66 million years ago; the third of three geologic periods from the Mesozoic Era

dwarf—an animal below average size

excavate—to dig in the earth

extinct—no longer living; an extinct animal is one that has died out, with no more of its kind

fossil—the remains of a living thing (like bones and teeth) or traces of its action (like footprints) preserved in the rock record

Jurassic Period—the span of geologic time from 200 to 145 million years ago; the second of three geologic periods from the Mesozoic Era

quarry—a place where stone or other minerals are dug from the ground

paleontologist—a scientist who studies fossils

rival—a person who tries to outdo or be better than another person

sauropod—a member of a group of closely related dinosaurs with long necks, thick bodies, and long tails

species—a particular kind of living thing

specimen—a particular individual or sample of something; in the case of fossils, a specimen is the remains of one particular example of a species

vertebra—a back bone; more than one vertebra are vertebrae

Read More

Brusatte, Steve. *Field Guide to Dinosaurs.* New York: Book Sales Inc., 2009.

Holtz Jr., Thomas R. *Dinosaurs: The Most Complete, Up-to-Date Encyclopedia for Dinosaur Lovers of All Ages.* New York: Random House, 2007.

McCurry, Kristen, illustrated by Juan Calle. *How to Draw Incredible Dinosaurs.* North Mankato, Minn.: Capstone Press, 2013.

West, David. *Brachiosaurus and Other Long-Necked Herbivores.* New York: Gareth Stevens Pub., 2011.

Internet Sites

Use FactHound to find Internet sites related to this book. All of the sites on FactHound have been researched by our staff.

Here's all you do:

Visit www.facthound.com

Type in this code: 9781491421239

ABOUT THE AUTHOR

Thomas R. Holtz Jr. is a vertebrate paleontologist with the University of Maryland Department of Geology. He has authored dozens of books and articles on dinosaurs for children and adults. He has even appeared in dinosaur-themed comic strips. A graduate of Yale and Johns Hopkins, Dr. Holtz lives in Maryland when he's not traveling the world, hunting fossils.

Index

Bibliography

Carballido, J.L.; Marpmann, J.S.; Schwarz-Wings, D.; Pabst, B. (2012). "New information on a juvenile sauropod specimen from the Morrison Formation and the reassessment of its systematic position." *Palaeontology* 55 (2): 567–582. doi:10.1111/j.1475-4983.2012.01139.

Carpenter, K. (2006). "Biggest of the big: a critical re-evaluation of the mega-sauropod Amphicoelias fragillimus." In Foster, J.R.; and Lucas, S.G. (eds.). Paleontology and Geology of the Upper Jurassic Morrison Formation. *New Mexico Museum of Natural History and Science Bulletin*, 36. Albuquerque, New Mexico: New Mexico Museum of Natural History and Science. pp. 131–138.

Carpenter, K. and Tidwell, V. (1998). "Preliminary description of a *Brachiosaurus* skull from Felch Quarry 1, Garden Park, Colorado." Pp. 69–84 in: Carpenter, K., Chure, D. and Kirkland, J. (eds.), The Upper Jurassic Morrison Formation: An Interdisciplinary Study. *Modern Geology*, 23 (1-4).

D'Emic, M.D. and B.Z. Foreman (2012). "The beginning of the sauropod dinosaur hiatus in North America: insights from the Lower Cretaceous Cloverly Formation of Wyoming." *Journal of Vertebrate Paleontology*, 32(4): 883-902. doi:10.1080/02724634.2012.671204.

Foster, John. *Jurassic West: The Dinosaurs of the Morrison Formation and Their World*. Bloomington, Indiana: Indiana University Press, 2007.

Gregg, Clifford C. (1964). "Memorial to Elmer S. Riggs (1869–1963)." *Geological Society of America Bulletin* 75 (9): 129–132.

Maier, Gerhard. *African Dinosaurs Unearthed: The Tendaguru Expeditions*. Indiana University Press, 2003.

Mazzetta et al., G.V. (2004). "Giants and Bizarres: Body Size of Some Southern South American Cretaceous Dinosaurs." *Historical Biology*: 1–13.

McIntosh, J.S.; Berman, D.S. (1975). "Description of the palate and lower jaw of the sauropod dinosaur *Diplodocus* (Reptilia: Saurischia) with remarks on the nature of the skull of *Apatosaurus*." *Journal of Paleontology* 49 (1): 187–199.

Paul, G.S. (1988). "The brachiosaur giants of the Morrison and Tendaguru with a description of a new subgenus, *Giraffatitan*, and a comparison of the world's largest dinosaurs." *Hunteria*, 2 (3): 1–14.